This book belongs to:

....

101 Dalmatians is based on the original book by Dodie Smith,
published by Viking Press

This is a Parragon book
This edition published in 2005

Parragon
Queen Street House
4 Queen Street
Bath, BA1 1HE, UK

Printed in China
ISBN 1-40545-941-7

Disney Storybook Collection

p

Contents

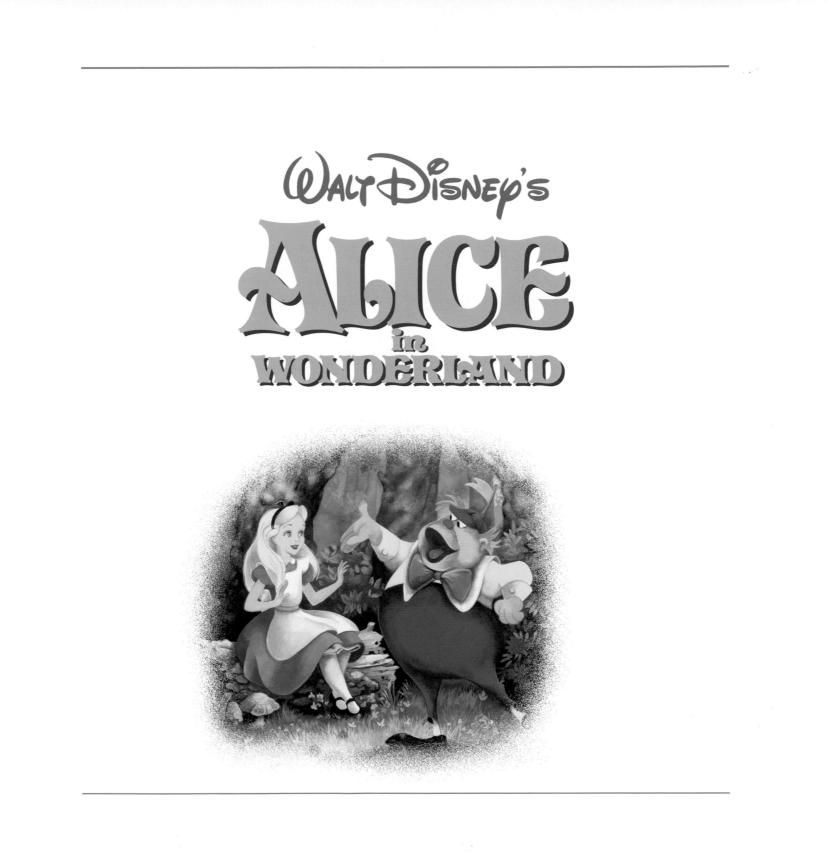

One beautiful spring day a young girl named Alice sat by the river listening to her sister read aloud from a history book. But Alice wasn't really listening. She was playing with her cat, Dinah, and daydreaming.

The sun was bright and the air was warm. Soon Alice began to close her eyes. She no longer heard her sister's voice.

Suddenly a large white rabbit dashed by. Alice jumped up. The rabbit was wearing a waistcoat and bow tie and was carrying a huge pocket watch. "I'm late! I'm late for a very important date," the White Rabbit muttered as he went along.

Alice went chasing after him, but stopped short at a rabbit hole.

The rabbit scuttled down the hole. Thinking he might

be late for something fun, like a party, Alice followed him.

Suddenly she stumbled and fell head over heels into the hole. But instead of falling faster, she began falling slower and slower – until she was floating.

She landed gently, just in time to see the rabbit disappear through a tiny door. Alice was too big to follow him. The Doorknob suggested she try the bottle on the table, which said "drink me". Alice drank and drank. With every sip, she got smaller and smaller.

When she was ready to open the door, the Doorknob told her that he was locked. Then he suggested she try a biscuit from the box labelled "eat me". Alice did and she began to grow. Soon she was crying giant tears. The Doorknob told her to drink again. She grew smaller and smaller until she could float right through the keyhole.

On the other side of the keyhole, Alice found she was in the strangest place. There were talking birds and walking fish, and a Cheshire cat who kept appearing and disappearing.

Alice kept hoping that one of these creatures could help her find the White Rabbit, but they were no help at all.

She came upon a pair of twins. They introduced

themselves as Tweedledum and Tweedledee.

"How do you do, Tweedledum and Tweedledee?" Alice greeted them. She could not tell them apart at all.

"When first meeting someone, you should shake hands and state your name and business," said Tweedledum, grabbing Alice's hand and shaking it firmly.

"That's manners!" said Tweedledee, grabbing her other hand and giving it a good squeeze.

With that, the twins danced Alice round and round. But they were so rough that they flipped her over, knocking her onto her back. Alice was not pleased.

"Talk about manners!" Alice exclaimed as she picked

herself up. "If you must know, my name is Alice, and I'm following the White Rabbit. I'm very sorry, but I must go."

Despite the twins'

protests, Alice went on her way. Soon she came to an unusual garden. Flying about were bread-and-butterflies and a rocking-horse fly. Alice discovered that the flowers of Wonderland could speak!

"What kind of flower are you?" a big orchid asked her.

"Oh, I'm not any kind of flower," Alice replied.

"Why, no fragrance at all," added another flower, sniffing her. Alice did not know what to make of this.

"Just as I suspected!" a rose cried. "She's nothing but a common weed!" The rose turned her back on Alice.

"Leave!" shouted the flowers. "We don't want you in our lovely garden." They pointed to the way out.

Feeling very upset, Alice was forced to run away.

Then, nearby, Alice saw a familiar grin up in a tree. It was the Cheshire Cat. She asked if he'd seen the White Rabbit.

"No," replied the cat. "But if I were looking for him, I'd ask the Mad Hatter." And with that, the cat began to disappear.

Alice realized that the cat hadn't told her how to find the Mad Hatter. She walked along and saw two road signs pointing in the same direction. One read "Mad Hatter" and the other read "March Hare".

She followed the signs to a clearing in the woods where the Mad Hatter was giving a tea party with the

March Hare. They made Alice feel quite unwelcome. They refused to offer her a cup of tea and had no intention of helping her find the White Rabbit.

Alice went on her way and soon ran into the Cheshire Cat again. She explained that she was trying to find her

way home. But the cat replied that all ways led to the Queen. He opened a door and Alice stepped through.

The White Rabbit hurried into view. He was about to announce the Queen! The Queen of Hearts appeared and invited Alice to play croquet. But during their game, the Cheshire Cat showed up and tripped Her Royal Majesty. The Queen was enraged and blamed Alice. "Off with her head!" she cried. There was a mad chase and Alice ran through Wonderland to get away.

Suddenly Alice awoke on the riverbank. "You've been

dreaming," her sister said.

Alice looked around but didn't see any strange talking creatures. All she saw were her sister, the old history book and Dinah, her cat. And that was just fine with Alice.

Pongo, Perdita and their fifteen puppies lived in a cosy little house in London. The house belonged to their humans, Roger and Anita. They were perfectly happy until they met Cruella De Vil – Anita's old schoolfriend who simply loved spotted puppies.

She wanted to buy them all and make them into spotted fur coats!

Roger put his foot down. "These puppies are not for sale and that's final."

Cruella was furious but she refused to give up.

One night Cruella's two nasty henchmen, Horace and

Jasper, kidnapped the puppies! Then they drove out to Cruella's old country estate and waited to hear from their boss.

When the puppies got there, they saw lots and lots of other Dalmatian puppies who had also been snatched by Horace and Jasper.

Back at home, Pongo and Perdita could not believe what had happened.

Perdita knew

at once that Cruella was behind her missing puppies.

"She has stolen them," sobbed Perdita. "Oh, Pongo, do you think we'll ever find them?"

Pongo knew that the Twilight Bark was their only hope. He would bark his message to the dogs in London.

They would pick it up and pass it along to the dogs in the country. And maybe someone would find the puppies.

That night the Twilight Bark reached a quiet farm where an old English sheepdog known as Colonel lay sleeping peacefully.

"Alert, alert!" shouted Sergeant Tibs, a cat who lived on the farm. "Vital message coming in from London."

The Colonel listened closely. "Fifteen puppies have been stolen!" he cried.

Sergeant Tibs remembered hearing barking at the old De Vil place. They headed straight for the gloomy mansion.

The Colonel helped Tibs look through the window. Sure enough, there were the fifteen puppies – plus their eighty-four new friends!

Tibs and the Colonel overheard Cruella, Jasper and
Horace talking. When they heard her plans to make coats
out of the puppies, they knew there was no time to waste.
The Colonel ran off to get word to Pongo and Perdita
while Tibs helped the puppies escape!

As soon as Horace and Jasper realized what was

happening, they tried to stop the puppies. But it was too late. Pongo and Perdita arrived and fought off the foolish thugs as the puppies hurried to safety.

Once all the dogs were safely out of the house, they

thanked the Colonel and Tibs and went on their way. A

black Labrador retriever arranged for them to ride to

London in the back of a removal van that was being

repaired. The dogs waited in a blacksmith's shop.

Suddenly Cruella's big car drove up the street. She

had followed their tracks and was parked and waiting.

But Pongo had a clever idea. There were ashes in the

fireplace. If they all rolled in them, they would be disguised in black soot. Then they could get aboard the van without Cruella  realizing it was them! And that's just what they did.

It worked perfectly until a blob of snow dripped onto a puppy and washed off a patch of soot. From her car, Cruella could see it was a Dalmatian puppy.

"They're escaping!" she cried as the van took off.

There was a really scary chase. Cruella tried to pass the van on the road, but she ended up crashing through a barricade and driving right into a huge pile of snow. Cruella's beautiful car was a wreck! And that wasn't all.

She had lost the puppies! Cruella threw a tantrum.

Pongo and Perdita and 99 puppies arrived home safely, much to Roger and Anita's delight. Roger pulled out a handkerchief and wiped Pongo's face clean.

"What will we do with all these puppies?" Anita asked.

"We'll keep them," Roger answered. He sat down at the piano and composed a song right on the spot. "We'll buy a big place in the country, and we'll have a plantation," he sang. "A Dalmatian plantation!"

And that's exactly what they did.

Walt Disney's

Lady and the
TRAMP

Lady was a happy little dog. She lived in a big house with Jim Dear and Darling. One day Lady learned that Darling was expecting a baby. Lady didn't know that

things in the house would soon be very different.

One day Lady met a scruffy dog named Tramp. Tramp had no home and no family. He went wherever he pleased and did whatever he pleased.

"Believe me," Tramp told Lady and her friends, Jock and Trusty, "babies change everything! Now you'll have nothing but trouble. Just wait and see!"

But Tramp was wrong. When the baby arrived, Lady had one more wonderful person to care for and love.

Several weeks later, Jim Dear and Darling went off on a trip. Aunt Sarah came to stay at the house. "Lady," said Jim Dear, "help Aunt Sarah take care of the baby."

Aunt Sarah brought her Siamese cats with her. They

made a lot of trouble. Lady
barked at the cats, but it
did no good.

"Shame on you, Lady!"
shouted Aunt Sarah.
"Attacking my poor little
angels. A muzzle is what
you need!" She took
Lady right to the pet
shop to buy one.

The muzzle was more than Lady could bear. She had
to run away. When Lady stopped to catch her breath, she

was in a strange part of town surrounded by a pack of mean dogs. Just then her friend Tramp appeared. Seeing that Lady was in danger, he fought the stray dogs and chased them off.

"You poor kid!" said Tramp, looking at the muzzle. He took Lady to the zoo, where a friendly beaver chewed right through the muzzle and freed Lady.

Afterwards, Tramp took Lady to visit one of his favourite places. They shared a romantic dinner for two at Tony's Italian restaurant.

Finally, after a lovely stroll through the park, Lady said, "I must go home. I promised Jim Dear I'd take care of the baby."

"Okay, Pigeon," said Tramp. "But let's have some fun first."

"Tramp, no!" said Lady. But Tramp had already rushed into a nearby yard to chase the squawking chickens.

Suddenly the dogcatcher appeared. Before she knew it, Lady was on her way to the pound without Tramp. Lady was ashamed and scared in the pound – especially when the other dogs began to tease her. A dog named Peg came to Lady's rescue. "Can't you see the poor kid's scared enough already?" Peg said to the other dogs.

The dogs were jealous because Lady had a shiny licence and would soon be going home.

When Lady finally came home, Tramp said, "I'm sorry I got you into trouble, Pidge." But Lady was too angry to listen. She refused to speak to Tramp.

Later that night, Lady saw a rat scurry up a vine to the

baby's room. She barked as loudly as she could.

When Tramp heard Lady barking, he came running.

"What's wrong, Pidge?" he asked.

When Lady told him about the rat, Tramp ran into the

house and up the stairs.

Lady pulled at her chain until it broke. Then she ran up to the baby's room to help Tramp fight the rat and save the baby.

"You vicious brutes!" cried Aunt Sarah when she saw Lady and Tramp in the baby's room. "Get away from the baby!"

Aunt Sarah called the dogcatcher to come and take Tramp away.

When Jim Dear and Darling came home that night, Lady helped Jim Dear find the dead rat.

"Lady," said Jim Dear thankfully, "I think you and your friend were trying to save our baby from the rat."

Meanwhile, Jock and Trusty went to find Tramp. They soon caught up with the dogcatcher's wagon. Trusty

began barking very loudly – so loudly, in fact, that he

scared the horses. They reared up and the wagon tipped

over right onto poor Trusty.

Trusty had a broken leg, but he would be just fine.

Lady and Jim Dear arrived just in time to free Tramp.

Jim Dear and Darling were so grateful to Tramp that they asked him to live with them always.

By Christmas of that year, Lady and Tramp had four puppies – and the family's happiness was complete.

Walt Disney's

MICKEY MOUSE

The Sorcerer's Apprentice

Long ago in a long-lost land there lived a man of magic. He was known far and wide as the Sorcerer. All the powers of the world were at his command: fire, water, wind and earth. There was nothing he could not do.

One day, a young lad named Mickey appeared at the door and begged to be taken on as the Sorcerer's apprentice.

"I have no time to teach you tricks," the Sorcerer muttered as he searched impatiently for his magic hat.

The Sorcerer was about to send him away when Mickey whisked a red silk scarf off a table. Beneath it was the Sorcerer's magic hat. "Is this what you are looking for?" Mickey asked.

At that, the Sorcerer realized that perhaps he could use a bright young apprentice.

Mickey soon set to work sweeping and mopping. Sometimes he would sneak away from his chores and secretly watch the Sorcerer at work. How he longed to be like the old man with his vast knowledge of spells!

Late one night, the Sorcerer removed his magic hat and placed it on the table. Then, as he went upstairs, he asked Mickey to do one last chore and fill the vat with water before he went to bed.

As soon as the Sorcerer was out of sight, Mickey picked up the magic hat and put it on just to see how it fit. Suddenly, Mickey felt a strange surge

and knew that now he had magical powers, too.

Spotting his old broom, the Sorcerer's apprentice took a deep breath and began to chant: *"Dooma, dooma, brooma, brooma . . ."*

Magically, the broom came to life, sprouting two arms of its own.

Mickey motioned for the enchanted broom to pick up two buckets and follow him to the fountain in the courtyard. There he directed the broom to fill the two buckets with water and carry them back to the  vat. Since the vat was quite large, Mickey had the broom continue to fetch more water.

Quite pleased with himself, Mickey settled back in the Sorcerer's big chair to enjoy a few minutes' rest. He soon fell asleep to the soothing sound of water splashing into the vat. . . .

In his dream, Mickey slowly ascended to the top of a pinnacle. Above him was a starry sky; below, a silken sea. With a flutter of his fingers, Mickey made the stars circle around his head like a crown of fire. Then he leaned over the water and drew the tides to him.

The waves were lapping at his feet. . . .

Mickey awoke with a start, waist high in water. The broom was still filling the vat with water! He watched in horror as the water came cascading over the rim!

"Stop!"
Mickey cried.
"Halt!" But the
broom neither
heard nor heeded.
In desperation,
Mickey picked up
an axe and broke
the enchanted
broom into
many pieces.

Mickey left the room and shut the door. But just then each of the broom splinters began to come alive! Soon there was an army of marching brooms – each with two buckets. Mickey heard the noise and opened the door a crack to peek outside. A parade of brooms trampled right over him!

As the brooms steadily poured more and more water into the vat, Mickey frantically bailed the water out through a nearby window. But it was no use. For every bucket he managed to bail out, each of the brooms poured in two more.

Whirling and swirling, the water swept Mickey off his feet and carried him away. Then the Sorcerer's

book drifted by. Mickey scrambled aboard the big book as if it were a life raft and frantically started searching for a spell to undo the damage.

Suddenly, a beam of white light pierced the darkness. Mickey looked up, and there, on the stairs, stood his master.

Slowly, the Sorcerer raised his arms. He murmured some words, thrust both arms straight out and pointed his fingers at the terrible torrent.

Instantly, the raging sea parted, and the waters began to recede. And when the last swirl of water had vanished, there Mickey stood, wet and shivering, in a shallow puddle.

As Mickey gazed up sheepishly, the Sorcerer stared down at him with cold, angry eyes. Mickey took off the magic hat and returned it to its owner. Then, with downcast eyes, he rushed off to complete his chores.

And so Mickey never even saw the sly little smile the Sorcerer flashed as he picked up the once enchanted broom. But from then on, the Sorcerer found a few minutes each day to teach his pupil the true uses of magic.

Long ago, in the city of London, there lived a family named Darling. Wendy, John and Michael Darling would sit in the nursery telling stories about a far-off place called Never Land, where the daring Peter Pan and the

pixie Tinker Bell lived. And no one in Never Land ever grew old.

Peter Pan and Tinker Bell came to the Darlings' nursery window one night to get his shadow. It wasn't Peter's first visit to the Darling house. He had come there many times to

listen to Wendy's stories. Peter was upset when Wendy explained that this was to be her last night in the nursery.

"But that means no more stories," cried Peter, "unless I take you all back to Never Land with me."

"That would be wonderful," the children shouted. Everyone but Tinker Bell agreed.

"But how will we get there?" Wendy asked.

"All you've got to do is fly," Peter replied.

And, with a sprinkle of pixie dust from Tinker Bell, they soared through the skies of London and all the way to Peter's Never Land home.

Down below they saw waterfalls and Mermaid Lagoon. There was a pirate ship, a forest and even an Indian camp.

The pirate ship belonged to a fellow called Captain Hook. The captain had two enemies in Never Land – Peter

Pan and a hungry crocodile. One day, in a fight with Peter, the crocodile had got a taste of Hook's hand and had followed him around ever since, hoping for more. Hook blamed Peter Pan.

When they got to Never Land, Peter took Wendy,

Michael and John into the forest to meet the Lost Boys.

Then he and Wendy went to visit Mermaid Lagoon.

There Peter spied the Indian Chief's daughter, Tiger Lily,

tied up in Captain Hook's boat. They heard Hook ask

Tiger Lily to reveal Peter's hiding place. But the Indian princess wouldn't tell him anything.

"I have to save Tiger Lily!" Peter cried. He and Wendy followed Hook to Skull Rock. Peter challenged the Captain to a duel. But Peter was too fast and too smart for Hook. With one quick lunge, the Captain landed in the water next to his greatest fear – the hungry crocodile.

Peter rescued Tiger Lily and brought her back to the Indian camp.

Captain Hook got away from the crocodile and swore revenge against Peter Pan. He kidnapped Tinker Bell and tricked her into telling him where Peter lived.

Then the pirates went to Peter's hideout and captured

Wendy, John, Michael and the Lost Boys.

Knowing that Peter would never be able to resist a beautifully wrapped package, the pirates left a present in the tree house for him. As soon as he opened it, BOOM, it would explode! And that would be the end of Peter Pan.

Tinker Bell knew what Hook had planned. She had to warn Peter before it was too late! She made her escape carefully and flew back to the hideout.

"Peter Pan will save us," Wendy insisted as she was

about to walk the plank.

But the evil captain just laughed at her. "Pan will never save you now!" he cried with glee.

Captain Hook did not realize that Tinker Bell was

already on her way to get Peter.

Peter and Tinker Bell returned in a flash. "Hook, this

time you've gone too far!" Peter shouted as he challenged him to one last duel.

Wendy, Michael, John and the Lost Boys watched in awe as Peter fought so bravely to save them. At last Hook and the pirates ended up in the water. They swam as fast as they could, with the always-hungry crocodile close behind.

"Thank you so much for saving us," said Wendy. "And now I think it's time for us to go back home."

Before they could say "Captain Hook", Peter set sail in Hook's very own ship through the skies of Never Land.

They were soon back in London safe and sound.

Peter and Tinker Bell said their goodbyes, and the Darlings promised never to forget the wonderful times they had. As the years went by, they would remember everything – Peter, Tinker Bell, the Pirates, Tiger Lily and the Lost Boys – just as if it had all happened yesterday.

DISNEY's
THE LITTLE MERMAID II

AN ICY ADVENTURE

Princess Melody did not know that her mother, Ariel, had once been a mermaid. Melody was just a baby when her parents took her out to sea to meet her grandfather, King Triton, ruler of Atlantica. King Triton had a gift for Melody: a locket that held images

of life under the sea, to remind her of the merpeople.

Suddenly, a crazy sea witch named Morgana showed up and tried to kidnap Melody!

King Triton drove Morgana away with his powerful trident, but, nonetheless, Ariel decided she would have to keep Melody away from the sea for her own safety.

Sadly, King Triton dropped the locket, letting it sink to the ocean floor.

As Melody grew older, her parents did not tell her about Atlantica. And Melody was forbidden to swim beyond the sea wall that surrounded the castle. Melody hated that rule! She loved the

sea and felt at home in the water. Sometimes she would

sneak through the sea wall to swim and play in the open ocean.

One day, Melody found a locket on the ocean floor. When she brought it home and opened it, a beautiful vision of a magical land of mermaids appeared! But then Ariel saw the locket and snapped it shut. It was the gift King Triton had wanted to

give Melody years ago, but Ariel could not tell her that.
She feared that Melody would be drawn to the sea and
put herself within Morgana's reach.

Feeling angry and hurt, Melody grabbed the locket

and ran out of the castle. Then she sneaked through the sea wall and rowed out to sea in a boat. If her mother would not tell her what the locket meant, Melody would find out on her own.

Morgana's shark, Undertow, was watching Melody. "Morgana's the best," he told her. "She'll help you." The young princess was fascinated. Morgana's manta rays pulled Melody's boat far out to the sea witch's hideout in an iceberg.

Morgana knew what Melody wanted to hear. "Deep down, you know you weren't meant to be a lowly human," said Morgana. "What you are is something far more enchanting. . . ."

Melody couldn't believe it. "A mermaid?" she

asked hopefully.

Then, with a drop of potion, Morgana turned Melody's legs into mermaid's fins. It was like a dream!

Melody never wanted to be human again, but Morgana warned her that the potion would wear off.

"I could make the spell last longer if I had my magic trident," the witch lied. "Oh, but it was stolen years ago. . . ." The sea witch was trying to convince Melody to steal King Triton's trident!

Little did Melody know that King Triton was her grandfather – and that the trident rightfully belonged to him, not Morgana. With the trident, Morgana would be ruler of the seas, and she could make the king and all sea creatures bow to her.

Melody fell for the trick. Soon the little mermaid was swimming towards Atlantica. On a nearby iceberg, she asked a penguin and a walrus – Tip and Dash – to help her find the way. "She's a damsel in distress!" said Dash. Diving into the water, the two would-be heroes led Melody to King Triton's palace.

Once there, she hid under a table, watching King Triton. "He doesn't look like a thief," Melody whispered. Still, with Tip and Dash's help, she took the trident when no one was looking.

Melody swam back to Morgana's hideout. Tip and Dash were at her side – until they caught sight of Undertow and swam off in fright. Melody was just about to hand the trident to Morgana when, suddenly, Ariel appeared – as a mermaid! Ariel's old friend, Flounder, was with her.

"Mum!" Melody cried out in surprise. "You're a mermaid?" Ariel tried to explain, but her daughter felt betrayed. "You knew how much I loved the sea," Melody said. "Why did you keep the truth from me?"

Melody still had no idea how evil Morgana was, or how hard her mother had tried to protect Melody from her.

"Please give the trident to me, Melody," Ariel said, pleading.

But it was no use. Melody gave the trident to Morgana, and the sea witch cackled with evil laughter.

She grabbed Ariel with one tentacle, then sealed
Melody and Flounder inside an ice cave. "Your mummy
was only trying to protect you from me," Morgana said.

Melody realized, too late, that she had been tricked!

As the sea witch rose to the water's surface, her spell over Melody wore off. Melody's fins turned back into legs, and she could not breathe under water. She was trapped below the surface in the ice cave!

Luckily, Tip and Dash returned just in time, rammed the ice wall, and freed Melody.

On an iceberg, Melody watched as Ariel and King Triton were forced to bow to Morgana under the power of the trident.

But the trident had no effect on Melody – she was human!

Quickly, Melody crept up to the top of a huge ice structure and surprised Morgana. They struggled over the trident.

Finally, Melody snatched it away and threw it to King Triton.

"Grandfather!" she cried out. "I believe this belongs to you!"

King Triton blasted Morgana with the trident,

sealing her forever in a block of ice. Melody was reunited with her family, and she hugged her grandfather for the first time.

As a gift to Melody, King Triton gave her a choice:

she could stay with him in Atlantica, or she could return to her home on land. But Melody had a better idea. She took the trident and zapped the sea wall that surrounded the castle. Now the entire family – merpeople and humans – could finally be together.

Long ago, deep in the jungles of faraway India, there lived a wise black panther named Bagheera. One day, as Bagheera sat in a tree, he saw something surprising. "Why, it's a Man-cub!" said the panther.

Bagheera was not able to care for the Man-cub, so he took the baby to live with a family of wolves.

The wolves named the little boy Mowgli and raised him as one of their own.

Ten rainy seasons came and went. Mowgli grew, and

no Man-cub was happier than he. The creatures of the

jungle were good to him.

But one jungle animal did not wish Mowgli well. It was Shere Khan, the strong and cunning tiger.

Shere Khan feared nothing but Man's gun and Man's fire. He was sure the Man-cub would grow up to be a hunter.

"Shere Khan has returned to our part of the jungle!" Akela the wolf said one day. "Surely

he will try to kill the boy." Mowgli was no longer safe.

"It is time for Mowgli to return to his own kind," Bagheera said. "I will take him to the Man village."

"Hurry," Akela said. "There is no time to lose."

Bagheera and Mowgli started on their way.

"We'll spend the night here," Bagheera said as they settled down on the branch of a tree.

Just then Kaa the snake appeared. He thought Mowgli would make a tasty morsel. The snake used his hypnotic eyes to put Mowgli in a trance. He wrapped the Man-cub in his coils.

Bagheera awoke just in time to smack Kaa on the head

and send him on his way. It was time to keep moving!

Mowgli decided he didn't want to go with Bagheera. "The jungle is my home!" the Man-cub insisted. He went off on his own.

Along the way Mowgli saw a parade of elephants. He thought it was wonderful and wanted to march along with them. But when it was time for the elephant inspection, Colonel Hathi took a closer look at Mowgli.

"What happened to your trunk?" asked the Colonel.
"Why – you're a Man-cub!" he cried.

Bagheera came to Mowgli's rescue. He insisted on
taking him to the Man village, but Mowgli refused once

more. "Then from now on, you're on your own!" Bagheera told him.

Mowgli soon met a good-natured bear named Baloo. Baloo helped Mowgli forget his troubles. They played together, swam together and ate sweet, ripe bananas and coconuts all day long.

As the two friends floated on the river, a group of monkeys swooped down on Mowgli. They picked him up and dragged him off to the ancient city of the monkey king.

The monkey king wanted

something from Mowgli.

"Teach me the secret

of fire," King Louie

demanded. "Then

I can be human

like you!"

Bagheera and

Baloo arrived in time

to help Mowgli escape from the monkeys. "Now you see

why you must leave the jungle!" they pleaded.

But Mowgli still did not believe his friends. He ran away

from them again – right into the great Shere Khan himself.

"I'm not afraid of you, Shere Khan!" said Mowgli bravely. A storm began to blow around them. Suddenly a bolt of lightning struck nearby.

The lightning started a small fire. Mowgli grabbed a burning branch and tied it to Shere Khan's tail. The terrified tiger ran away, never to be seen again.

As Mowgli proudly walked through the jungle with his friends, he heard a new and beautiful sound. It was a girl from the Man village, singing a sweet song.

Mowgli couldn't look away. He stopped walking to listen. "Go on, Mowgli!" Bagheera urged. "Go on!"

Mowgli knew that he must follow the girl and her song. She smiled at Mowgli as he walked with her all the way to the village. He turned to wave goodbye to his friends.

Baloo and Bagheera watched Mowgli leave. Their hearts were sad, but they knew it was as it should be. Their Man-cub had found his true home at last.

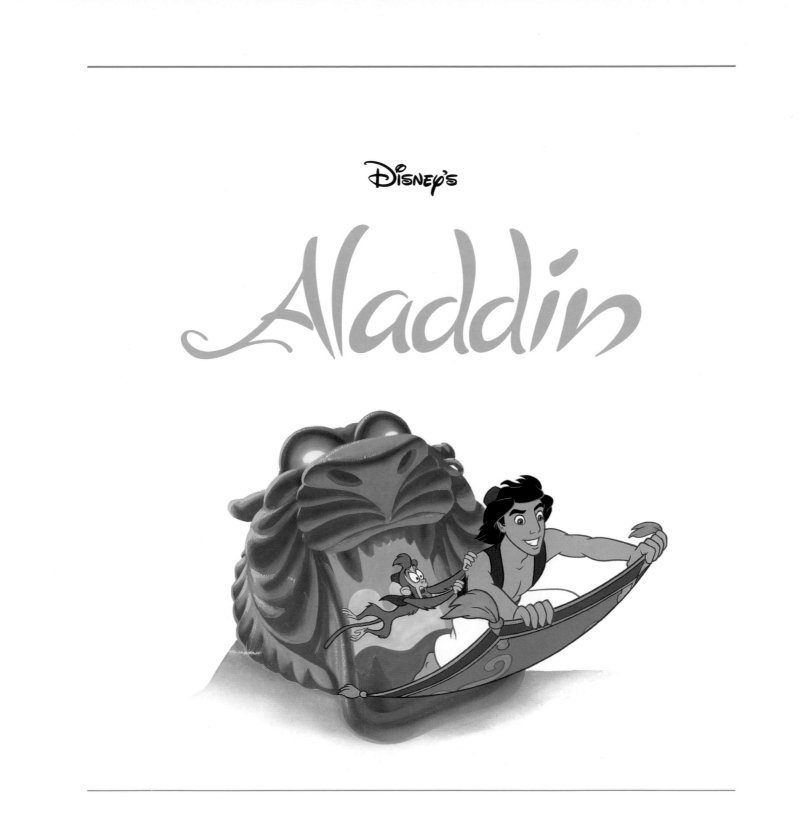

Long ago, in a faraway land called Agrabah, there lived a poor orphan named Aladdin. One day in the market, Aladdin took some bread for his dinner. The Sultan's guards chased him, but Aladdin and his pet monkey, Abu, escaped. Then Aladdin saw two hungry

children and gave the bread to them. "Things will change," he promised Abu. "Someday we'll live in a palace!"

That afternoon at the palace, Princess Jasmine was told by her father, the Sultan, that she must marry a prince in three days. Jasmine was very unhappy. "I will marry only for love!" she cried.

Jasmine told Rajah, her pet tiger, that she would have to leave the palace.

Disguising herself in an old peasant robe, the Princess ran away. Tired and hungry, Jasmine took an apple from a stall in the market, but couldn't pay the angry fruit seller. Aladdin came to her rescue. The mean merchant called the guards. They released the Princess, but took Aladdin to the palace dungeon.

Meanwhile, Jafar, the Sultan's evil adviser, disguised himself as a prisoner. "Help me find a very special lamp," he said to Aladdin, "and I'll set you free."

Jafar took Aladdin and Abu to the Cave of Wonders. A magic carpet appeared and led Aladdin to the lamp. But just as Aladdin reached for it, Abu grabbed a large, sparkling jewel.

The cave began to collapse. The magic carpet saved Aladdin and Abu, but all three were

trapped. "What's so special about this old lamp?" Aladdin wondered aloud. As Aladdin rubbed the dusty lamp, an enormous genie appeared.

"Master," he said, "I can grant you three wishes, but

you can't wish for more wishes. Now let's get out of here!"

Aladdin's first wish was to become a prince so Jasmine would want to marry him. But he promised to save his last wish to set the Genie free.

Later that day, Aladdin arrived at the palace in grand style, introducing himself as Prince Ali Ababwa. Later that

evening Prince Ali took Jasmine for a ride on his wonderful carpet. The Prince looked very familiar. "Aren't you the boy from the marketplace?" asked Jasmine.

"No, I'm Prince Ali," Aladdin insisted, even though he knew he wasn't being honest.

Then the magic carpet took them back to the palace.

"That was just wonderful," sighed Jasmine. She had fallen in love.

Aladdin was thrilled that things finally seemed to be going his way.

But suddenly the Sultan's guards, under orders from Jafar, appeared and grabbed poor Aladdin. After they tossed him into the sea, Aladdin summoned the Genie and used his second wish

to save his own life.

Aladdin returned to the palace with the lamp, but Iago, Jafar's parrot, stole it, and Jafar became the Genie's master.

"Make me Sultan," Jafar commanded.

"And make the Princess and her father my slaves."

The Genie was forced to obey. The poor sultan was hanging from his throne room like a puppet watching

Jafar take over his kingdom. He also had to watch his daughter wait on Jafar's every whim.

Jafar used his second wish to become an all-powerful sorcerer. He changed Aladdin back into a beggar and sent him far away. Aladdin thought he was doomed until the magic carpet appeared and helped him return to the palace. Jafar was furious, but Aladdin found a way to trick him.

"The Genie still has more power than you'll ever have," he told Jafar.

This infuriated Jafar and he used

his third wish to become a genie. But he forgot one important thing. Genies become the prisoners of their lamps, shackled to them for all time. Jafar disappeared into a glowing black lamp.

To Jasmine's delight, the Sultan decided to let the

Princess choose her own husband. And there was only one choice for Jasmine – Aladdin.

Now it was Aladdin's turn to make someone happy. He turned to the Genie and said, "I wish for your freedom." And that was the best wish of all!

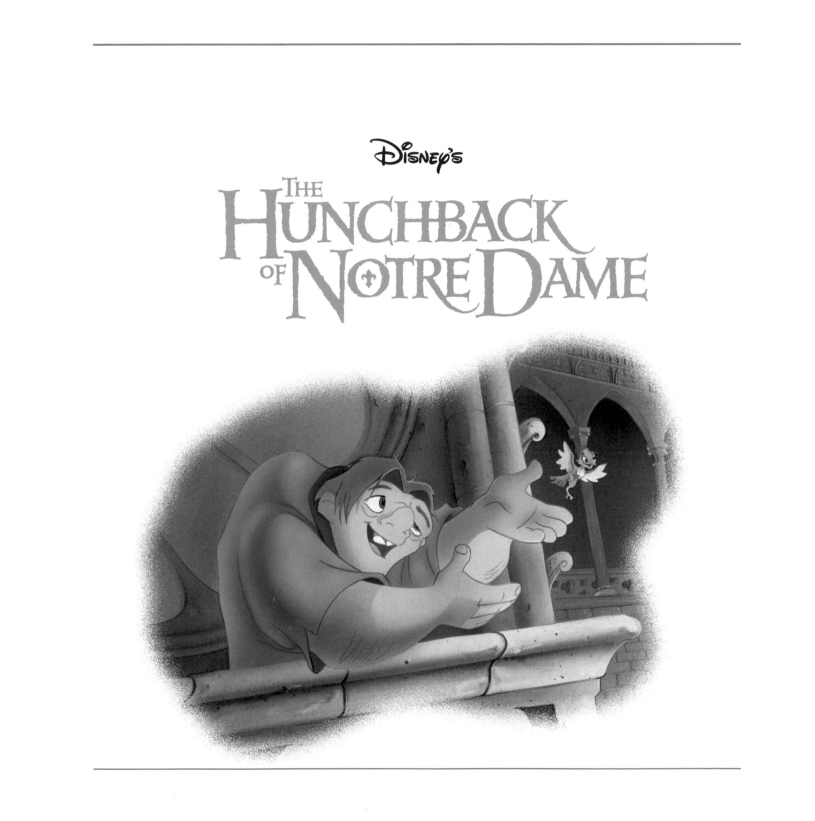

Long, long ago in the city of Paris, a young, odd-shaped man lived up in the bell tower of the great Cathedral of Notre Dame. He was the bell ringer Quasimodo. His name meant "half-formed", and had been

given to him by his cruel master, Judge Claude Frollo. Quasimodo's only friends were the stone gargoyles that came to life in his small world.

Quasimodo longed to walk in the city below his tower, but the pris... ...ho forbade it. He was a mean man who hated everything and everyone – especially gypsies. He had even

convinced gentle Quasimodo that he was a monster, and

that terrible things would happen if he went out among

the people.

Once a year, all of Paris prepared for a great festival.

On that day, known as the Festival of Fools, the people

paraded around the city dressed in scary masks and

hoped to be crowned the King of Fools. The gargoyles

told Quasimodo that this year he must attend the festival.

Everyone was so
busy having a good
time, no one noticed
the poor bell ringer
wandering around.
He met the dancing
gypsy, Esmeralda,
and thought she was
beautiful. So did

Phoebus, Frollo's new Captain of the Guard, who rode into Paris that same day.

When Quasimodo was crowned King of Fools, the people laughed. They threw ropes over him to hold him down. Frollo would not rescue Quasimodo, but Esmeralda ran to cut Quasimodo free.

Frollo was enraged. He ordered Phoebus to arrest her.

But Esmeralda and her grey goat, Djali, ran into the cathedral where she knew she would be safe. Frollo's soldiers could not touch her once she was inside. But Frollo warned her, "Set one foot

outside these walls, and you're my prisoner!"

Quasimodo did not understand. He believed that all

gypsies were bad, but Esmeralda was good and kind and gentle. His master had been wrong. Maybe Frollo had been wrong about him, too. Maybe he wasn't a monster!

Quasimodo decided to help Esmeralda escape.

Quasimodo carried Esmeralda and Djali down the side of the cathedral. When they got to the street, she gave him a special amulet to keep. "Use this if you ever need help," she explained. "It will lead you to the Court of Miracles, where you can find me." Then, promising to visit him soon, Esmeralda vanished.

Meanwhile, Phoebus convinced Esmeralda that he

was on her side – not Frollo's. When Phoebus refused to obey the judge, Frollo ordered his soldiers to kill the Captain. Phoebus was injured and fell into the river, where he was left for dead. Hiding by the

bridge, Esmeralda saw everything. She rescued Phoebus and asked Quasimodo to hide him in the bell tower.

Quasimodo sadly agreed, for he could see that the two

were in love. Soon Frollo came to the bell tower, hoping

to trick Quasimodo into telling him where Esmeralda was

hiding. He convinced Quasimodo that he already knew

about the gypsies'
hideout, the Court of
Miracles, and planned
to attack at dawn.

Quasimodo and
Phoebus set out to
warn Esmeralda
about Frollo's plans.
Using the amulet,

they found their way to the Court of Miracles. They did not realize something very important: they were leading Frollo and his soldiers there, as well.

"Take them away!" Frollo cried. They were all his prisoners now.

But chains could not hold the determined bell ringer. Quasimodo escaped and rescued

Esmeralda. Phoebus, the gypsies, Quasimodo and the

gargoyles fought bravely against Frollo and his soldiers.

When the battle was over, the trio walked out of the

cathedral and into the sunlight smiling. Quasimodo was cheered by the crowd. The bell ringer who once thought he was a monster was now a great hero!

Walt Disney's

MICKEY MOUSE

BRAVE LITTLE TAILOR

Once upon a time, there was a tailor named Mickey. He lived in a kingdom ruled by a good king and the beautiful Princess Minnie. All was well in the land until a terrible giant appeared. The king offered a rich reward to the one who could get rid of the giant.

"Have you ever killed a giant?" the butcher asked the baker.

Before the baker could answer, Mickey declared, "I killed seven with one blow!"

Now, Mickey was talking about flies, not giants. But he was called before the royal court. And before he could explain that he had killed seven flies, not giants, Mickey was appointed Royal Giant Slayer.

Mickey was sent to work right away. He went out into the country in search of the giant. As it turned out, the giant was not hard to find. What *was* hard was staying out from under the giant's great big feet!

"Yikes!" cried Mickey, leaping into a cart of pumpkins.

"Food!" exclaimed the giant, reaching for the pile of pumpkins.

To the giant, pumpkins were no bigger than grapes. He popped them into his mouth. And he popped Mickey in, too! Oh, no! Mickey was trapped in the giant's mouth!

To wash down his pumpkin snack, the giant tore a well right out of the ground. As he drank, the water flowed from the well into the giant's mouth,  carrying with it the well bucket, still tied to the well. Thinking quickly, Mickey grabbed hold of the bucket. When the giant finished his drink and took the well from his lips, out came the bucket. Mickey was free!

Now the brave little tailor had a plan. Mickey

leaped from the bucket onto the giant's arm. Then he

slipped under the giant's shirt and crawled up his sleeve.

A giant hand chased Mickey into the sleeve. Mickey used his tailor's scissors to cut his way out.

When the giant's hand followed him out of this new hole, Mickey went to work and sewed it up again.

The giant's hand was caught in his own sleeve!

Finally, Mickey swung round and round the giant, hanging onto the end of the long length of thread. Within moments, Mickey had the giant all tied up.

When the giant tried to get away, he stumbled and fell. The terrible giant hit his head and passed out. Soon he was snoring soundly. Then Mickey tied the giant up with strong ropes so he couldn't get away.

The brave little tailor had neatly sewn up the giant problem. His reward was one million golden pazoozahs. And, in the eyes of Princess

Minnie, it certainly didn't hurt that the brave little tailor was the kingdom's biggest hero.

Naturally, both Mickey and Minnie lived happily ever after.

The End

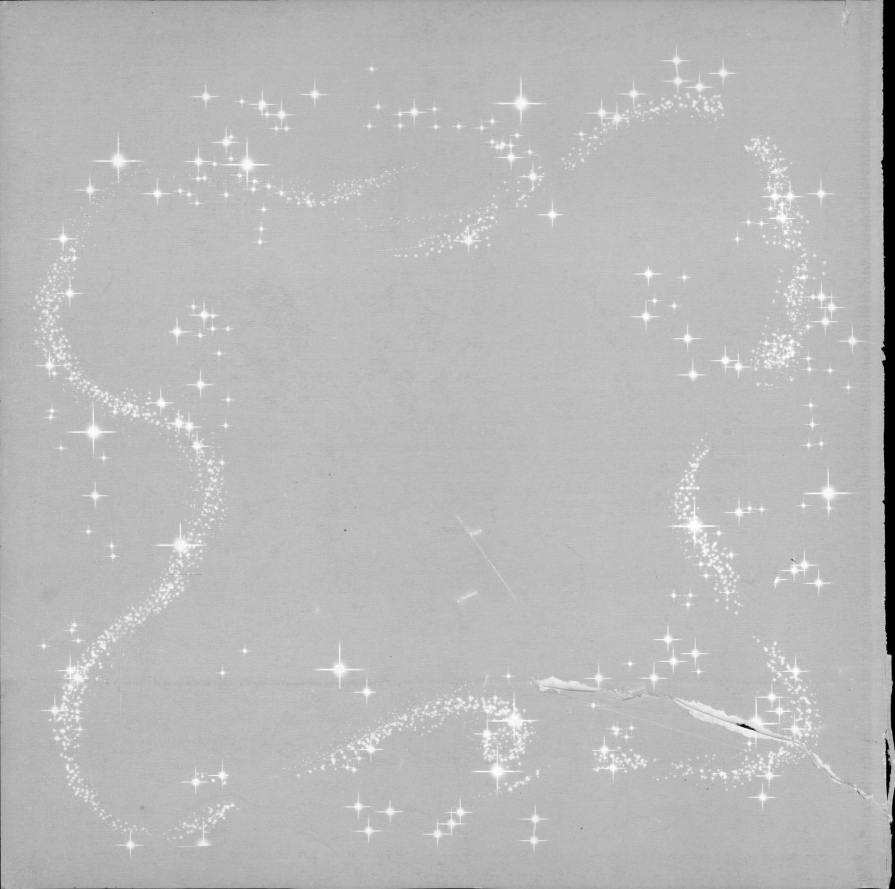